T0326088

FOO
LEG

BUKAYO
SAKA

BEN LERWILL

Published in the UK by Scholastic, 2024
1 London Bridge, London, SE1 9BG
Scholastic Ireland, 89E Lagan Road, Dublin Industrial Estate, Glasnevin,
Dublin, D11 HP5F

SCHOLASTIC and associated logos are trademarks
and/or registered trademarks of Scholastic Inc.

ISBN 978 0702 33326 2

A CIP catalogue record for this book is available from the British Library.

Printed and bound in Great Britain by Clays Ltd, Elcograf S.p.A

Paper made from wood grown in sustainable
forests and other controlled sources.

FSC
MIX
Paper | Supporting
responsible forestry
FSC® C018072
www.fsc.org

1 3 5 7 9 10 8 6 4 2

While this book is based on real characters and actual historical events,
some situations are fictional, created by the author.

www.scholastic.co.uk

FOOTBALL LEGENDS

BUKAYO SAKA

SCHOLASTIC

Contents

4, DECEMBER 2022

It was a warm night in Qatar. Bukayo had three lions on his shirt and a big-match feeling in his stomach.

He breathed deep and joined his teammates in the tunnel. He felt calm and focused, but part of him was dizzy with excitement. Here under the stands, he could hear the buzz of the crowd and the swell of the pre-match music. Two lines of players – one from England, the other from Senegal – waited in silence. Soon, it was time.

"Come on, boys!" shouted Jordan Henderson behind him, as the two teams began walking out and the stadium roared to life. "Let's do this!"

More than 65,000 fans had packed into the ground, but Bukayo knew that the world was watching too. Tens of millions back home in England, hundreds of millions around the planet. This was a huge match, the kind he had always dreamed about.

England had got to the World Cup knockout stages. Tonight, they were hoping to win and reach the quarter-finals.

Senegal were a great side, with big names from top clubs, but England were confident. In the changing room, their manager Gareth Southgate had reminded them that no other country at the tournament had scored more goals or earned more points. If they played well, Gareth said, this would be their night.

When the whistle blew, Bukayo felt ready. He was playing as part of a front three, with Phil Foden and captain Harry Kane. But early in the game, it was Senegal who had the chances. Only some good fortune – and the saves of goalkeeper Jordan Pickford – kept the score at 0-0. In the stands, the England fans started getting nervy.

Then, after thirty-eight minutes, things changed. Harry and Jude Bellingham combined on the left to set up Jordan Henderson in the box, who fired home.

YESSSSS! 1-0! A delighted Bukayo ran across to congratulate them.

Things got even better just before half-time, when Jude and Phil played in Harry to score a second. 2-0! The fans went wild. "What a brilliant move!" shouted the TV commentators. The team felt more relaxed. They were winning – it was happening!

At half-time, chants rang around the stadium. But in the changing room, Gareth was clear. "This match is not over!" he said, looking his players in the eyes. "Don't take anything for granted. Go out there and give it everything!"

Bukayo was determined to do just that. Back out on the noisy pitch, he ran and worked tirelessly. He knew that if England could just get one more chance to score, a three-goal lead would make things safe.

Twelve minutes into the second half, Harry set Phil free on the left. Phil burst forward at speed, leaving behind a defender, then played a low cross into the area. The stadium held its breath. Here was the chance England needed – but would there be anyone on the end of it?

There would be. And he knew exactly what to do.

It took less than two seconds for the ball to reach

Bukayo, but in his head, time seemed to slow down. He was able to judge the speed of the cross. He was able to think about where the goalkeeper was. He didn't panic. When the ball arrived, he simply used his left foot to lift it coolly over the keeper and into the net.

GOOOOAAAALLLL! 3-0!

As the roars of celebration echoed around the world, Bukayo's teammates ran over to mob him. He felt as though he would never stop smiling. Here he was, just twenty-one years old, and he'd scored the goal that was sending England through to the World Cup quarter-finals. He pointed into the night sky as the fans in the stadium sang his name.

What a feeling!

Bukayo's path to stardom had not always been easy. But one thing was certain, he thought, as the chants of the crowd rang in his ears. He had come a long, long way from the back garden.

GARDEN GAMES

The six-year-old boy put the ball on the grass and stepped back, sticking his tongue out in concentration.

He and his older brother had been in the garden for two hours, practising their passing and taking shots at each other. He had scored goal after goal – but he wanted more. He ran up and swung his left foot at the ball, sending it whistling past his brother and between the garden goalposts.

"Yaaayyy!" shouted the boy.

"OK," said his brother, who was two years older. He loved football too but was getting tired. "Can we stop now, Bukayo?"

"Not yet! Not yet!" said Bukayo. "Pleeease stay out with me, Yomi!"

Placing the ball back on the grass, he moved back and took another run-up. This time, though, it went high over Yomi's head, sailing over the bushes and out of the garden.

"Noooo!" Bukayo sighed, suddenly sad. "We'll never get that back."

Yomi shook his head and walked inside. "This is exactly what happened last week," he said.

"Sorry, Yomi." said Bukayo. "I really hope Dad can get us another ball."

The two boys lived with their parents in Ealing, West London. Their mum, Adenike, and their dad, Yomi Senior, had moved to London from Nigeria years earlier. When their youngest son had been born – in Ealing, on 5 September 2001 – they named him Bukayo, which means "bringing more happiness" in Yoruba, one of the languages in Nigeria.

It was through Yomi Senior that his sons inherited their love of football. Their dad had been a good player in Nigeria, and even though he lived in London, he had become a big fan of Newcastle

United. "When I first saw Alan Shearer play on TV, I just knew I had to be a Newcastle fan," he explained to the boys. "What a striker!"

Two days after Bukayo had lost the ball over the bushes, Yomi Senior came back from work holding a bag from a sports shop. The boys saw the bulge inside the bag and their eyes lit up. "Here you go." He tossed them their new ball as they cheered. "Just be more careful this time. Maybe put the goal against the fence instead of the bushes."

Bukayo and his brother were back outside within seconds. When there was a ball to be played with, the two boys were in the garden every day, rain or shine. They both had natural talent and, in Bukayo's case, endless energy too. The ball never got bored or tired, thought the boy, so why should he?

Often, Bukayo would simply refuse to end the game if he wasn't winning. The way he saw it, football was fun, but it was even more fun when he was ahead. Time and again, if he was losing, he would plead to carry on playing. Winning made him feel good, even when there was just his brother and his dad to play against.

As the brothers played outside with the new ball,

Adenike and Yomi Senior chatted in the kitchen. "Those two are football mad," Adenike said with a smile. "They are," said her husband, chuckling. "Particularly Bukayo – even when he's not in the garden, he's out on the green, dribbling the ball up and down. Let's find a local club for him to join. Football makes him happy."

A few minutes later, a young face appeared in the doorway. It was Yomi.

"Dad," he said, looking a bit nervous. "Bukayo has been practising his shooting. He's kicked the ball so hard that he's broken the fence."

A BRIGHT
TALENT

When Yomi Senior asked his friends and family about local football teams, one name came up quickly.

"Take him to Greenford Celtic," said Bukayo's uncle, enthusiastically. "They're a grassroots club for young players. They have an Under-7s team."

Bukayo loved this idea, so the next day, when he came back from primary school, Yomi Senior drove him to where Greenford Celtic trained. Bukayo packed his trainers and even took his best water bottle. He was buzzing with excitement.

When they arrived, they could see dozens of kids

in green-and-white hooped shirts practicing on the pitches. The head coach at the club was a friendly man called Colin – but he looked apologetic when Yomi Senior asked if Bukayo could join.

"I'm really sorry," he said. "We're completely full."

Bukayo's face fell. His dad, not knowing what to say, thanked Colin and started walking his son back to the car.

"Hang on a moment," said Colin, who could see how upset they were. He looked down at Bukayo. "Seeing as you're already here, would you like to join in with our training session today? Just as a one-off?"

The next hour was a joy for young Bukayo. He didn't have the right shirt, but he definitely had the right attitude. First he had to sprint across the pitch with the other players. Then he had to dribble a ball around cones. Finally, and best of all, he had to play in a practice match.

By the end of the hour, Colin looked shocked. He went over to speak to Yomi Senior on the sidelines.

"Wow," he said. "Your son's a brilliant little player. He's fast, he's skilful and he works really hard. I've been chatting to the other coaches and we think we can try to make space for him in the squad."

Bukayo jogged up and appeared at his dad's side, holding his water bottle. He was out of breath and happy. "Did you hear that?" said Yomi Senior. "Colin would like you to join the club. What do you think?"

The boy's face lit up. He looked ecstatic. "Yes, please!" he shouted.

Over the next few months, Colin wasn't the only one to be amazed by Bukayo's skill and determination. The big professional clubs in and around London all had scouts who kept an eye on local football teams. Soon, these scouts began to talk about the six-year-old boy at Greenwood Celtic who played with a smile on his face and dynamite in his boots.

His teammates loved having him in the side. During one game he chased back, made a tackle, then played a one-two before scoring past the keeper! "Yes, Bukayo!" cried his teammates, patting him on the back.

It wasn't long before Yomi Senior and Adenike started hearing from big clubs, inviting Bukayo in for trials. Watford were in touch, then Chelsea, Spurs and even Arsenal! They could barely believe it. Only a few months ago, Bukayo had proudly pulled on his

Greenford Celtic Under-7s shirt for the first time. Now he was attracting the attention of professional scouts all across London!

Because Watford was the closest club to where the Saka family lived, Bukayo went there first. To make it even better, his brother Yomi had recently started training there too.

The day when his dad dropped him off at Watford's Harefield Academy, Bukayo was amazed. It had a huge indoor pitch under a curved modern roof. He stared at the goals and training equipment. Boys his age were kicking balls around, wearing club tracksuits. Yomi had told him about the training complex, but seeing it with his own eyes was special.

Someday soon he knew he would be trying out at even bigger clubs. But for now, this was heaven.

FINDING A
NEW CLUB

Bukayo's parents were proud of him, but they knew how important it was for him to stay level-headed. "Enjoy your football," Adenike told him one night, as she sat on his bed, "but never stop being you." For Bukayo, being himself was simple. He still enjoyed all the things he normally did – joking with his schoolfriends, eating home-cooked food, playing outside until it was dark – and he never grumbled if he had to help with chores. When he had pocket money, he spent it on Twix bars and football magazines.

Some weekends, Yomi Senior would let his

sons stay up to see *Match of the Day* on TV with him. They loved sitting together and watching the star players, but there was one in particular who fascinated Bukayo. "Look at Cristiano Ronaldo," he said, as they watched a replay of the Manchester United striker finishing off a team move. "He's like a magician."

Bukayo's time at the Watford academy was helping him improve as a player. The coaches showed him how to get better at crossing and heading the ball. Even though he was still so young, he was learning that being in a team was about working hard and linking up play.

It also helped that some of the other players at the academy were brilliant. Bukayo thrived when he was on the same team as a skilful boy a year older than him, called Jadon Sancho.

By now, Bukayo was seven. Every weekday he put on his red school jumper and went to join his friends at Edward Betham Primary School. Bukayo had a cheeky laugh and a big sense of fun, but he always paid attention in class. Some of the lessons he learned from the teachers were the same as the lessons he was learning from football. Try your hardest. Compete fairly. Take pride in what you do. The similarities made sense to the young boy.

Life was busy for Bukayo, with academy sessions and practice matches to go to, but he didn't mind one bit. The more chance he had to play football, the better. Already, though, his mind was turning to bigger things.

Playing and training at Watford was great, but he also knew that the academies of London's top Premier League clubs were still interested in him. He would be sad to say goodbye to Jadon and his other Watford friends – and Yomi would miss him – but maybe it was time to move on.

Bukayo's talent meant he could take his pick from three massive clubs. It was only later in his life that he realized how amazing this was – a primary-school boy being scouted by not one, not two, but three Premier League academies! But for now, he had a decision to make. His mum and dad wanted their young son to be able to choose the academy that suited him best.

He visited them all. The first club, Chelsea, had won lots of trophies in recent years, but their academy pitches were a long way from Ealing.

The second club, Spurs, had modern facilities and exciting players but they were struggling in the league.

Then he visited the third club. Bukayo's spirits soared when he saw the training complex, especially when the staff told him about the exciting style of play they coached. It felt just right, and when Yomi Senior brought him to a trial training session, his mind was made up. "This is the one, Dad!" he said as he got back in the car. Bukayo imagined himself wearing the club shirt, and the thought made him glow inside.

Above the training academy was a big red badge with a golden cannon.

The club he had set his heart on was Arsenal.

YOUNG
GUNNER

Soon afterwards, on 5 May 2010, Bukayo signed his first official forms with Arsenal Football Club. He was eight-and-a-half years old. No one knew then what his story would be, and none of the older children arriving that morning paid much attention to the little player shaking hands with the coaches. One day, however, they would all know his name.

A few weeks later, three boys were playing on the green in front of the Saka family house. "Van Persie's through! What a finish!" shouted Bukayo, pretending to commentate as he jinked past his cousin Folu and hammered the ball past Yomi. They all laughed as

Bukayo ran to fetch the ball.

Ever since he'd joined the Arsenal academy, Bukayo had tried to copy the tricks and skills of the first-team players. He was already dreaming of what the future might hold. One minute he'd imagine he was striker Robin van Persie, the next he'd be winger Theo Walcott, or midfielder Jack Wilshere.

Jack was a real inspiration for Bukayo. On the walls of Arsenal's Hale End training complex were photos of some of the youngsters who had come through the academy and become first-team players. One of them was Jack. He had joined the club in 2001, aged nine, and was now one of Arsenal's star midfielders. He was even part of the England set-up too! Bukayo looked at Jack's photo every time he arrived for training. It showed him that dreams could come true.

From the first moment he stepped into Hale End, Bukayo had felt at home there. He was one of the youngest boys in the whole academy, but this made him excited rather than nervous. The coaches always made sure the sessions were fun. Bukayo enjoyed them so much that whenever he came home from the academy, he gulped down a glass of juice then went straight back outside to carry on playing!

The coaches were impressed with Bukayo, too. It was clear straight away that he had the skills and character to go a long way. He was growing, too, and becoming stronger.

One day, academy coach Trevor Bumstead was talking to Liam Brady, the head of Arsenal's youth development. They were standing by the Under-10s training pitch, watching the youngsters play. "Young Saka is definitely one to keep an eye on," said Trevor.

Liam had been an Arsenal legend, playing more than 200 times for the club, so he knew talent when he saw it. As the two men watched, Bukayo received the ball, skipped down the wing and sent a beautiful cross to the far post. A minute later, he sprinted half the length of the pitch to meet a through-ball, which he chipped over the keeper and into the net. Liam whistled softly. "One to keep an eye on indeed," he said, smiling.

In his bedroom that evening, Bukayo flicked through the latest copy of his football magazine. As he turned the pages, the magazine fell open at a photo of the Arsenal team in their new 2010/11 kit.

His eyes widened as he looked along the rows

of faces. There was Jack. There was Robin, who had been top scorer last season. And there was the captain, Cesc Fabregas, who had moved over from Spain as a teenager to join the academy at Hale End.

Arsenal were one of the biggest clubs in England. Their manager, Arsène Wenger, had been there for almost fifteen years, so far winning the Premier League three times and the FA Cup four times. Yomi Senior had told Bukayo all about incredible players like Tony Adams, Thierry Henry, Dennis Bergkamp and Freddie Ljungberg, who had carried Arsenal to glory. It all made Bukayo feel proud to wear the badge.

And not just proud, but determined. He had been told that only a tiny number of the youngsters at Hale End would go on to become first-team players, but he wanted to make it more than anything. He was still staring at the poster when Adenike came into his room to turn his light out.

"Goodnight, Bukayo," she said, coming across to him. "Sleep well."

"Night, Mum," he replied.

Before his light went out, he took one last look at the photo of the players in their smart red-and-white shirts.

Keep working hard, he thought. One day – just maybe – that might be me.

HALE END ACADEMY

Arsenal's Hale End Academy, in north-east London, is a big part of what makes the club so special.

Over the decades, lots of players have come through the academy to become first-team stars.

They include Liam Brady, David O'Leary, Tony Adams, David Rocastle, Ashley Cole, Cesc Fabregas, Jack Wilshere, Emile Smith Rowe, Eddie Nketiah and, of course, Bukayo!

The academy has teams from Under-9s through to Under-16s, for both boys and girls. The youngsters go to school during

---

the day then to Hale End to train in the evenings. To begin with, the players are given an eight-week trial to show what they can do. If they make the grade, they're invited to officially join their age-group.

The academy has things that it considers to be the most important skills for a young footballer. They're known as the Four Pillars. The first is to gain a good school education away from the pitch. The second is to understand the importance of movement and making the right runs. The third is to stay dedicated and determined, even when things aren't going well. The fourth is to be a team player. The current (2023) manager of the academy is Per Mertesacker, who played more than 150 times as a centre-back for Arsenal between 2011 and 2018.

A TASTE OF
THE BIG TIME

Early one Monday morning in the summer holidays, Yomi Senior had a surprise for his sons. The boys were watching a Spongebob Squarepants cartoon, but he made them turn off the TV and told them they would all be driving up to Manchester that day.

"But why?" asked Bukayo, confused.

"Because ..." said Yomi Senior, with a big smile, "Newcastle are playing at Manchester United tonight – and we have tickets!"

The brothers' jaws dropped. Then they started running around the house, whooping and hollering.

They were going to watch a Premier League match!

It felt like a dream. The afternoon was a blur of motorways and service stations, but by 8 p.m. that night, the Saka family were in their seats in a crowd of 75,000, watching on as the players walked out on to the Old Trafford pitch. They were sitting in the away end, with all the Newcastle fans, and the noise was deafening.

Yomi Senior's beloved Alan Shearer had retired a few years ago, and Cristiano Ronaldo had moved away from Manchester United, but the pitch was still full of superstars like Wayne Rooney and Paul Scholes. It might not have been an Arsenal game – but what an experience!

Manchester United won 3-0, but the result didn't really matter to Bukayo. He just sat there soaking it all up. The atmosphere. The floodlights. The green, green grass. The brightly coloured kits. The roar of the crowd.

He watched the clever runs, the quick flicks and the mazy dribbles. He applauded the sliding tackles, the bullet headers and the curled free kicks.

"Just imagine playing in a stadium like this,

boys," whispered Yomi Senior to his sons.

Bukayo smiled to himself. It was as though his dad was reading his mind.

SCHOOL
SUCCESS

Mrs Curzon looked around the playground.

She was in charge of the football team at Edward Betham Primary School. But although they had a match coming up, she was struggling to find enough players in the top few years. Who could she ask?

Her eyes fell on Yomi Saka. He was already on her list, but maybe he could suggest someone else. Mrs Curzon knew that Yomi was a talented young player. She'd heard he was even playing at the Watford academy. She was sure he would have some ideas for extra players.

"Hello, Yomi," she said, walking up to him.

Yomi stopped playing football with his classmates. "Hello, Mrs Curzon," he replied.

"Now as you know," Mrs Curzon continued, "we've got a match next week in the Ealing Peal Shield, the big local cup competition. The problem is we still need a couple more good players. Can you think of anyone?"

Yomi gave a laugh and looked across at the smaller children on the other side of the playground. There was Bukayo, chasing around with some of his friends.

"Yes, I can," he said. "My little brother."

Mrs Curzon had to admit she was surprised by Yomi's suggestion, but when she watched Bukayo play, his name went straight on the team sheet. He was four years younger than the oldest boys in the school, but his skills were fantastic. When she chatted to him and found out he was training at the Hale End academy, she was amazed. A young Arsenal player, here at Edward Betham Primary! And, she thought, what a modest boy not to be shouting about it.

Despite his age, Bukayo handled himself very well in the Ealing Peal Shield match. So well, in fact, that although his school didn't win the trophy that term, he became part of the team for the next four years.

By the time those years had passed, Mrs Curzon and the rest of the staff knew all about Bukayo. He was hard-working and caring in class – and although he was a superb footballer, he was never big-headed.

With Bukayo as their star player, Edward Betham Primary won the Ealing Peal Shield in 2012 and 2013. He scored so many goals, and created so many assists, that when he left the school, the teachers retired his number ten shirt in his honour.

Bukayo's football journey was only just beginning, but already he was leaving his mark. And – just as importantly – he had his first two winners' medals for his bedroom shelf.

GROWING
UP

It was midway through the second half, and Arsenal were in trouble. The club's Under-12s squad had travelled up to Leeds to take part in a Premier League five-a-side tournament. They had reached the final, against Chelsea. The coach Luke Hobbs wanted to give all his players a chance to take part, so he played one team of five in the first half and a different team of five in the second.

The match had started well for Arsenal. Bukayo had played in the first half, helping Arsenal to a 3-0 lead. But when the team was rotated in the second half, Chelsea came back hard. Suddenly, it was 3-3! Luke and the Arsenal players started to get worried. "If we want to win," said Luke to his assistant, "we need to get Bukayo back on".

The boy was more than ready. Sprinting back on to the pitch, he got involved straight away. A minute later, he fired a shot home. Arsenal were back in the lead. Two minutes after that, he scored again to make it 5-3. Even on a small five-a-side pitch, with lots of touches and quick passes, the Chelsea players just couldn't get the ball from Bukayo. And as the clock ticked down, he curled another shot into the top corner. 6-3! Arsenal had won the trophy!

"Amazing, Bukayo!" shouted his teammates.

Life at the academy was full of rewarding moments, but it had its ups and downs. Every season, some of the players in his year group were released. Bukayo hated it when this happened, as they were often his good friends, but it made him realize how lucky he was.

He couldn't control the future, but right now, he was wearing an Arsenal shirt every week. He was a Gunner. And he would never take that for granted.

Bukayo did, however, have another problem. He was becoming taller by the month, which was good in some ways but bad in others. He was getting growing pains, which meant his heels and knees hurt when he was playing. This was hugely frustrating. It felt as though he was being stopped from doing what he loved.

"I still want to play all the time," he said to his coaches, "but it's painful when I run. How long is it going to be until I feel normal again?"

They always told him the same thing: be patient. And slowly, week by week, month by month, things became easier. The pain started to soften. He was so relieved when he felt fit again that he became even more determined on the pitch.

The coaches had known for years that Bukayo had all the right talents: pace, commitment, strength and skill. But now, they were delighted to see, he was also developing his football brain. He was learning how to find space, how to pull defenders away from his teammates, and how to choose the killer pass.

As time went by, Bukayo kept improving. One day, Liam, Trevor and the head coaches watched him playing for the Under-13s. He was tearing the opposition to shreds with his speed and shooting, so the coaches had an idea. To help him get even better, he would be moved to the year group above.

Soon, Bukayo was playing with older boys again. He was used to playing up front, but now he was asked to be a left-back. Some young players would have grumbled about this. Bukayo just got on with it, knowing the experience would help him. At Arsenal, no matter what the age group, the full-backs had to work hard for the rest of the team, running up and down the line for ninety minutes.

Some young players found this too difficult. But for Bukayo? No problem. He knew that the more effort he put in, the greater the reward.

Whenever he pulled his football boots on, he always knew what he had to do: give one hundred per cent for the badge.

A PRIMARY SCHOOL VISIT

After Bukayo's performance at Euro 2020, the staff and students at his old school, Edward Betham Primary, were so proud of him that they had a special mural painted in the playground, showing Bukayo's face.

They were thrilled when Bukayo himself came to visit and say thank you! "Special feeling going back to my primary school yesterday," he wrote on social media.

"Just a few years ago I was in the same shoes of all the kids who are young with big dreams, and I hope my return will remind them to believe they can achieve anything!"

GREENFORD
HIGH SCHOOL

After leaving Edward Betham Primary School, Bukayo had started at Greenford High School. It was just ten minutes from his front door, so he and his brother walked together to the school gates every morning in their ties and blazers. Their conversation usually focused on one thing – football.

"Ronaldo scored another hat-trick for Real Madrid on Sunday! He's having a dream season," said Yomi one autumn morning. It was another busy day in West London. Cars and buses whizzed past.

"He's like a machine!" agreed Bukayo, as the brothers spotted some of their school friends on the opposite pavement and waved. "He does it time and time again. That's the thing, Yomi – it's about consistency."

Bukayo was now fourteen. Each summer, he and the rest of the family would often be lucky enough to have a few weeks away – sometimes visiting Nigeria to see their relatives, or travelling across to the US, where Bukayo had cousins. But for the rest of the year, the pattern was the same: study hard at school, work hard at the academy. And, of course, play football at both. It was a routine that he loved.

At Arsenal, he continued to help his teams win youth tournaments and trophies. The same was true at Greenford High School. Sometimes he would play twice in a day – once at school, once at Hale End!

His sports teacher, Mr Harvey, was amazed at how Bukayo seemed to be as determined in the classroom as he was on the football pitch. Not only was he winning matches for the school, he was also working hard for his GCSEs.

At the same time, Bukayo's obsession with Arsenal was growing and growing. He had a new favourite Gunners star now – the powerful Chilean striker Alexis Sánchez. "Sir, did you see the highlights of the game this weekend?" he asked Mr Harvey at the end of a PE session. "Sánchez was on fire! He can score in so many ways. Volleys, free kicks, headers. He's so good!"

The teacher, who was an Arsenal supporter too, laughed. "He's amazing. And if you keep doing what you're doing, the fans might say the same thing about you one day."

People said this sort of thing a lot to Bukayo. It always made him happy, but he knew how important it was not to get carried away. The truth was, though, that his performances at the academy were getting better and better. The coaches were seriously impressed with his progress at the club – and they weren't the only ones.

One afternoon, he came home from school to find a letter waiting for him. His mum handed it to him with a smile on her face. It was only when he looked at it properly that he noticed the badge on the envelope.

Three lions in a white crest.

His heart started racing.

Tearing open the letter, he read it through. Then he read it through again, just to be sure.

"I've – I've been selected for the England Under-15s squad!" he shouted, holding out the sheet of paper for the rest of the family to read. The Saka kitchen was a noisy one that afternoon. Bukayo barely stopped smiling for the rest of the week.

His journey had always been a remarkable one – but now he was really going places.

A "NEARLY" MOMENT

Bukayo felt butterflies in his stomach as he made the long walk to the penalty area. It was two years later, in May 2018. He had graduated up to the England Under-17s and was playing at the UEFA Under-17 European Championships. It meant the world to him to be part of this team. Just a season earlier, his old Watford friend Jadon Sancho had been playing for this age group. The year before that, one of the young players he'd always admired at the Hale End academy – Emile Smith Rowe – had done the same.

Now it was Bukayo. And he had a job to do.

The tournament was being held on home soil.

England had made it as far as the semi-finals, where they were playing the Netherlands in a knockout tie at Chesterfield FC's stadium. Bukayo was playing at left-back, and several of his Arsenal teammates were also in the matchday squad: Vontae Daley-Campbell, Tyreece John-Jules and Folarin Balogun.

The match had finished 0-0. Time for a penalty shoot-out.

Five players had already stepped up. Two from England, three from the Netherlands. All of them had scored. Next up was Bukayo.

He placed the ball on the spot and stepped back. He knew his family were in the stands, looking on, but his only thoughts were about scoring. He relaxed. Then he stepped forward and – *bang!* – smashed the ball low into the corner.

He'd scored, but as he jogged back to the halfway line, he wasn't celebrating. England hadn't won yet. Sadly, just a few minutes later, that became impossible. Folarin missed his penalty, sending the Netherlands through to the final.

Folarin was devastated. Bukayo was one of the first to go up and comfort him. "Don't worry, Fol," he said to his friend. "That can happen to anyone. You played so well out there today."

An hour later, Bukayo met his family outside the ground. His brother came up and consoled him. "Well played, bro," he said. "We're all proud of you." Yomi had left the Watford academy and was now studying at university, but he remembered exactly how tough it was to lose a big match.

"It'll make you stronger," he said to his younger brother. And even in his disappointment, Bukayo knew that was true.

A HUGE
YEAR

One month later, Bukayo pressed the "off" button on the TV remote control, feeling deflated. Along with twenty-six million other people around the country, he and his family had just watched England lose the semi-final of the 2018 World Cup in Russia. The squad had done brilliantly over the past few weeks, led by players like Harry Kane and Raheem Sterling. The whole nation had been excited. But now, in the semi-final, they'd been beaten 2-1 by Croatia.

"Such a shame," Yomi Senior said with a sigh. Next to him on the sofa, Bukayo stared at the empty screen and wished he could somehow change the result. England had done the country proud. The manager, Gareth Southgate, had really motivated his players. But it wasn't to be. So close, yet so far. Another "nearly" moment.

He still felt inspired, though. The players had given everything, and he felt a particular connection to Raheem. Like Bukayo, Raheem was a young Black boy from London who had worked incredibly hard to succeed. To see him on a stage as big as a World Cup semi-final made Bukayo feel more confident in himself.

And as 2018 continued, he soon had lots of other reasons to feel confident. At the end of August, he received his GCSE results. His mum and dad had always told him how important it was to get good grades in case his football journey came to an end. And after dedicating so much time to revising and studying, he was thrilled when he got four A*s and three As. His parents were delighted for him.

"An A* in PE, my favourite subject," said Bukayo to his mum, happily. "I know that will make Mr Harvey pleased."

But the year's real highlights were still to come. Just after his seventeenth birthday, the moment arrived that Bukayo had dreamed about for years. He was offered a full-time contract by Arsenal! This was it. The big step up. He would be leaving Hale End after almost a decade and joining the Under-23 squad at the London Colney training complex – where the first team practised! Suddenly, his hopes for the future seemed within reach.

The club now had a brand-new boss, the Spanish manager Unai Emery, who had taken over after the end of Arsène Wenger's long time in charge. The squad, meanwhile, had stars like French striker Pierre-Emerick Aubameyang and World Cup-winning German midfielder Mesut Özil.

But Bukayo wasn't looking that far ahead just yet. In the meantime, he would be working with one of his heroes: Freddie Ljungberg, once a flying Arsenal winger and now the Under-23s coach.

Freddie had helped Bukayo for years, giving him words of advice and encouragement when he was at Hale End. And it was Freddie who had persuaded the other coaches that the teenager was ready to join the Under-23s. "He's good enough, I know it," Freddie had said. "He's coming up and training with me. I'll show he can play."

Bukayo didn't let him down. From the first match, he played with his usual commitment. He made clever decisions, his passing was accurate and he wasn't afraid to be physical. Just ten minutes into his debut match, against Manchester City Under-23s, he had his first assist! He might have been young, but he was playing like a pro.

Even better was to come at the start of November, when he lined up in a match against Chelsea Under-23s. With two teams full of highly talented players, it was Bukayo who opened the scoring, finding the back of the net then being swarmed by his teammates. And although the Gunners lost the match 5-4, Arsenal's young left winger had caught the eye of someone important.

Freddie took him to one side a few days later. "I have some news, Bukayo," he said, smiling. "Your performances have been great so far this season – really great. Unai Emery has just come to speak with me. The first team squad are flying over to Ukraine for a Europa League match next week. He'd like you to join them."

Bukayo thought he must have misunderstood. "Join them?" he said.

"As a squad member," said Freddie, slapping him playfully on the arm. "Congratulations!"

As he left London Colney that day, Bukayo felt as though he was walking on air.

ARSENAL FOOTBALL CLUB

Founded: 1886

Previous Names: Dial Square, Royal Arsenal, Woolwich Arsenal

Nickname: The Gunners

Most appearances: David O'Leary (722 appearances)

All-time Top Scorer: Thierry Henry (228 goals)

Ground: Emirates Stadium (capacity 60, 704)

Previous Ground: Highbury (from 1913 to 2006)

A DEBUT
FOR BUKAYO

When Arsenal kicked off against Vorskla Poltava on a cold Ukrainian night in late November, just 7,751 fans were in the stands. For the seventeen-year-old substitute on the bench, however, it was the biggest game of his career so far. Even in the pre-match warm-up, when he was passing balls back and forth with international stars like Aaron Ramsey, it felt like a dream.

"OK, everyone, listen," said Unai in the changing room before kick-off. "Vorskla are one of the best teams in Ukraine. This is a European tournament match, and we need to play with a positive attitude.

We have to work hard – no careless mistakes." He looked around at the squad. "Now let's go out there and win."

Arsenal's starting line-up that night had three players that Bukayo knew from the academy: Emile Smith Rowe, Joe Willock and Eddie Nketiah. They were all older than him, but the familiar faces helped him feel comfortable. He tried not to feel nervous as he watched from the dugout. Luckily, Emile and Joe both scored first-half goals to help Arsenal into a 3-0 lead. "Yessss!" shouted Bukayo on the bench.

At half-time, Unai gave another team talk. But as the players left to begin the second half, the manager tapped Bukayo on the shoulder and said, in a quiet voice: "Get ready to go on midway through the second half, OK?" The boy nodded and smiled, trying to act calm as a million thoughts raced through his head.

On sixty-eight minutes, it happened. At a break in play, Aaron was substituted and Bukayo was brought on, with the number eighty-seven on his back. He, Bukayo, was replacing the great Aaron Ramsey! The two players high-fived at the sideline. As he ran on to the pitch, Emile gave him a grin and a thumbs-up. Eddie called across to him too, shouting, "Let's go, Bukayo!" And just like that, after all the years of work, his first-team debut was underway.

There were no more goals to celebrate but he played a lively part in Arsenal's win, at one point even coming close to scoring. He certainly did well enough to impress Unai. Back in London two weeks later, the manager got all the players together to announce the starting line-up for the next Europa League tie, at home against the Azerbaijan club, Qarabag.

"Martinez... Koscielny... Özil... Nketiah... Lacazette..."

The list went on, until to Bukayo's amazement he heard the final name on the team sheet.

"...Saka."

He nearly fell off the changing-room bench. No way! A full debut – and at the Emirates Stadium!

If the substitute appearance in Ukraine had been a dream, this was a fantasy. He would be starting for Arsenal in front of the home fans! The night before the match, he thought of nothing else. "We're so proud of you! So proud!" his mum and dad kept saying. "You show them what you can do, Bukayo!"

Less than twenty-four hours later, he was lining up in the tunnel before the game. Walking out to a crowd of nearly 60,000 for the first time, under the glow of the floodlights, was an experience he would never forget. He looked around at the stadium where so many legendary players had played. What a moment – and he was still only seventeen! As the whistle blew, he blocked out the crowd and went into game mode.

He played with bravery and commitment, dribbling, passing, running and chasing. Just eight minutes in, he took a shot that nearly bent inside the post. So close! The fans soon warmed to the young winger flying around the pitch. And during the first half, Alexandre Lacazette fired Arsenal ahead. 1-0!

Bukayo kept the intensity up in the second half. After seventy-five minutes, he beat his man on the left, looked up and whipped a cross in. There was Eddie to head it home! A goal – but no! The offside flag was up. Stay positive, thought Bukayo. Keep working.

And another chance came soon. In the eighty-eighth minute, Arsenal broke away down the right.

Bukayo sprinted into the box, all alone. When the ball came across, it was just him and the keeper. Was this his moment? The crowd rose to its feet. Bukayo took one touch, paused, then belted it at the goal. Saved! So close again!

He hadn't scored, but Arsenal had won – and the TV crews all wanted to speak to the seventeen-year-old who had sparkled on the wing. "It's a dream come true," he told the interviewer on the pitch. "I want to thank all the coaches, and the fans that supported me. I should have scored at the end though!"

The interviewer asked him how his family had reacted when he was selected. "They were buzzing! They just couldn't stop smiling last night," he said. "We were all just so happy. But they managed to put me to bed early so I could focus on today!"

Bukayo made yet another appearance for the first team a few weeks later, as a late substitute in a Premier League game against Fulham, rounding off an unbelievable few months. As well as playing three times for the first team, he had finished the season with six goals and eight assists for the Under-23s. And because he was still so young, he had also had time to score another eight goals and two assists for the Under-18s! He was the talk of London Colney. There was no doubt about it. Bukayo had arrived!

ONWARDS AND UPWARDS

With five minutes left on the clock, the Einfracht Frankfurt fans were getting noisy. The summer had flown by. It was a few weeks into the 2019-20 season, and Arsenal were playing an away match in Germany in front of 47,000 fans. The Gunners were winning 1-0, but the home fans wanted an equalizer.

Arsenal's left-winger had other ideas. It was shortly after his eighteenth birthday, and he was back in the first team, now wearing the number seventy-seven shirt. He'd had a great match, keeping the defenders busy and setting up the game's only goal so far. But things were about to get even better.

In the eighty-fifth minute, as drums and chants echoed around the stadium, Arsenal stopped a Frankfurt attack and charged forward. The ball fell to their new big-money signing, Nicolas Pépé, who looked up and saw Bukayo in space. Suddenly, the ball was at Bukayo's feet, thirty yards from goal. He took two quick touches – the first to control the ball, the second to roll it forward – then curled a perfect shot into the corner.

GOOOALLLLL! His first for Arsenal! The away fans jumped for joy as Bukayo and his teammates ran across to them. "What a goal, Bukayo! Well done, mate!" shouted the captain Granit Xhaka.

Back in London, Bukayo knew just what he wanted to do with his shirt from the Frankfurt game. This had been his first really big moment in the team. The match had meant so much to him, and to his family and friends, but he also knew what it meant to Luke, Trevor and the other coaches at Hale End. So he framed the shirt and presented it to them as a gift, to help inspire other young boys and girls at the academy – just like he'd been inspired by Jack Wilshere all those years earlier.

Bukayo had a good feeling about this season.

Soon he was given his first Premier League start, in a 3-2 win against Aston Villa, and just a week later he was named in the team to face – wow! – Manchester United at Old Trafford. As the teams walked on to the famous pitch and the 73,000-strong crowd roared, Bukayo looked across at the away fans, where he and his dad had watched Newcastle so long ago.

Life was a whirlwind sometimes, Bukayo thought. It seemed like it was only yesterday when he was an unknown boy working hard for his dreams. Now those dreams were coming true. It gave him an amazing sense of achievement.

And amazing was how he felt in the second half when – with Arsenal 1-0 down – he played a neat ball through to Pierre-Emerick Aubameyang to equalize. An assist at Old Trafford – and more importantly, an away point for the team!

When he arrived for training at London Colney a few days later, he was spotted by the young Arsenal fans looking for autographs and selfies with players. "Saka! There's Saka!" they shouted, dashing across and crowding around with smiles on their faces.

As he patiently signed his name and posed for

selfies, Pierre-Emerick walked past them and gave Bukayo a wink. "This is a future superstar, kids!" he said to the young fans.

Pierre-Emerick was one of the big characters in the Arsenal squad, and he was always wowed by Bukayo's skill. In team training sessions, he would watch in disbelief as Bukayo fired in shot after shot from the edge of the box.

"Wow, you are on fire!" He smiled. "Like a little chilli!"

Bukayo and the rest of the squad laughed. As the season progressed, and Bukayo kept playing well, the nickname stuck: Little Chilli. He liked it.

But there was change coming – in more ways than one. First, Unai was sacked after a poor run of results, with former Gunners midfielder Mikel Arteta coming in to replace him as manager. Then, in early 2020, the Covid-19 pandemic swept across the world. Suddenly, fans weren't allowed in the stadium.

It meant that things felt different as the season went on. Bukayo wasn't yet an automatic choice for the first team – he was still so young, after all – but he was getting more and more game time, often at left-back. New manager Mikel soon realized how good Bukayo was. It didn't seem to matter whether there was a crowd there or not – whenever he pulled on a red shirt, Bukayo made a difference.

As the season approached its end, with Arsenal nowhere near the top of the Premier League but doing well in the FA Cup, Mikel made a decision. "Bukayo," he said after training one day. "The club would like to offer you a new long-term contract. We want your future to be here at Arsenal."

Bukayo was thrilled, and just a few days later he was celebrating again. In the forty-third minute of an away game at Wolverhampton Wanderers, with the score at 0-0, Arsenal full-back Kieran Tierney sent a cross in from the left. It hit an opposition player and bounced up, right into the path of Bukayo. He adjusted his body, pulled back his left foot and sent a glorious volley zooming into the net. 1-0! His first Premier League goal!

He was now fast becoming a fan favourite, recognized wherever he went.

There was more to come from Arsenal that season. At an empty Wembley Stadium, two goals from Pierre-Emerick saw the Gunners beat Chelsea

2-1 in the FA Cup Final. Bukayo was an unused substitute, but he was overjoyed to be part of a trophy-winning squad.

He finished the season with twelve assists – more than any other player in the squad – and four goals. And what was more, Little Chilli had an FA Cup winners' medal.

But he wasn't done yet.

ANOTHER WONDER YEAR

In the 2020-21 season, Bukayo's career went into hyper-speed. To his astonishment, he was handed the number seven shirt. This was one of the most important at the club. He would be following in the footsteps of legends like David Rocastle, Robert Pires and his old favourite Alexis Sánchez. What an honour!

"All those games in the garden finally paid off!" joked a delighted Yomi when Bukayo told him. "My little bro, the Arsenal number seven!"

The season began with more success, as he set up a goal for Pierre-Emerick in Arsenal's FA

Community Shield win against Liverpool. Then, less than a week later, he made his debut for the England Under-21s against Kosovo, starring in a 6-0 win alongside his clubmate Eddie and other talented youngsters like Sheffield United's Aaron Ramsdale and Borussia Dortmund's Jude Bellingham.

But that was just the beginning. Over the next month, to the delight of the fans, he started getting a regular spot in the Arsenal team – and before long he had yet more good news.

One afternoon after training, as Bukayo was relaxing at home, his phone rang. He didn't recognize the number.

"Hello, this is Bukayo speaking," he said when he answered.

"Hi Bukayo, it's Gareth Southgate here."

Bukayo sat bolt upright.

"Listen," continued the England manager. "I was impressed by your under-twenty-ones debut last month, and you've been playing brilliantly for Arsenal. I'd like you to join the first-team squad for next week's friendly game against Wales."

Bukayo was almost speechless. Was this really happening? His Arsenal teammates were delighted for him, and when Yomi Senior and Adenike found out, their faces filled with joy. "Incredible!" said his dad, "Just incredible! Congratulations, son!"

It was only when Bukayo lined up at Wembley the next week that it felt real. It was a friendly, and Covid-19 meant the stadium was still deserted, but here he was, starting for the actual England team! He thought back to his England Under-16s call-up. To be standing here just three years later seemed like a miracle. Determined not to let his country down, he put in a solid performance to help them win 3-0, thanks to some great play by Jack Grealish.

"Well played, Bukayo," said Gareth after the match. "You'll have many more chances to shine, I know."

The words filled him with hope. For now, however, his focus was on playing the best he possibly could for Arsenal. Under Mikel, there was an upbeat feeling in the club. Bukayo loved being in the same squad as people like his academy friend Emile and Brazilian defender David Luiz, who always had time to help the younger players. Bukayo now felt accepted, not just by his teammates, but by the millions of fans who were following Arsenal from home during the pandemic.

So he kept doing what he did best – giving everything on the pitch. In December, after performances that included a wonderful lobbed goal against Chelsea, the fans named him Player of the Month. This was the best Christmas present he could ever have wished for. It spurred him on to keep playing well, which meant he was named Player of the Month again in January – and in February too!

The fans' messages of praise and support arrived in their thousands on social media. Bukayo was becoming a true Arsenal star. By now, he had been able to buy a new house to live in with his parents. He had left Ealing behind – but only in some ways. In his head, he was still the same small boy who played football at every spare minute. He even still liked Twix bars!

The difference was that now, he was a professional player at one of the top teams in the country. Arsenal's league performances had been up and down this season, but by April they were still in with a chance of a trophy. They had made it to the quarter-finals of the Europa League, the tournament in which Bukayo had made his debut.

They were up against the Czech team Slavia Prague. Over two legs, Bukayo was far too good for their left-back, Jan Boril. The defender just couldn't keep up with the speedy Arsenal winger. When Boril lunged one way, Bukayo went the other. When he hung back, Bukayo ran circles around him. Arsenal drew 1-1 in London but won 4-0 in Prague. Through to the semi-final! "Boril's going to be having nightmares about you!" Emile joked as they left the pitch.

Sadly, the semi-final – against Spanish side Villarreal – was a bitter disappointment. The Gunners lost the first leg 2-1 in Spain. And despite trying everything in the second leg at the Emirates Stadium, they simply couldn't score. When the final whistle blew, Bukayo was massively frustrated. Noooo! They'd missed out on the chance of a final. The changing room was full of long faces.

The worse news was that Arsenal finished eighth in the Premier League, meaning they wouldn't even be playing European football next year. Only the fact that Bukayo had been named Arsenal's Player of the Season gave him something to feel happy about.

Then, one morning, his phone rang again. This

time, he recognized the number.

"Hi, Bukayo," said Gareth. "How do you fancy being part of the England squad for the Euros this summer?"

EUROS
DRAMA

Euro 2020 had been postponed for a year due to Covid-19, but when it finally arrived, it was a carnival of football.

All the biggest teams in the continent were playing, including France, Germany, Spain, Italy, Croatia and, of course, England. The matches were being held in cities right across Europe, with the semi-finals and the finals all at London's Wembley Stadium. What an opportunity for the Three Lions!

For Bukayo, just being part of the squad was beyond his wildest dreams. At the first training session, he felt starstruck when he looked around.

Harry Kane! Raheem Sterling! Marcus Rashford! He was the only Arsenal player selected in the twenty-six-man squad, but he was thrilled to see his old Watford academy mate Jadon in the group too.

They gave each other a warm hug when they met up. "It's so good to see you, bro!" said Bukayo.

The two soon realized they were part of something special. The team spirit was brilliant from their first day at St George's Park, England's base in the Midlands. The players seemed happy and confident, sharing jokes and training hard.

Excitingly, they would be playing all three of their group games at Wembley, against Croatia, Scotland and the Czech Republic. And although huge sell-out crowds still weren't allowed, about 20,000 fans would be at each match. What a difference that would make!

In England's first two games, Bukayo watched on from the sidelines. The Three Lions beat Croatia 1-0, thanks to a tidy finish from Raheem. A great start! A few days later against Scotland, however, they could only manage a disappointing 0-0 draw. Never mind. England were unbeaten and still on course to qualify for the Round of 16.

But they needed a lift, so when Gareth named his side for the Czech Republic game, Bukayo was on the list!

He was buzzing. Representing his country at a major tournament would be the ultimate honour. He was enjoying being part of the squad at St George's Park, and now he would be lining up with players that he admired not just as professionals, but as friends: Harry, Raheem, Declan Rice, Luke Shaw, Kalvin Phillips, Jack Grealish, Jordan Pickford. It all felt so special.

Bukayo was happy to see someone else on the team sheet, too. Playing for the Czech Republic at left-back was Jan Boril, the defender he had turned inside-out in the Europa League! And after Raheem headed England into an early lead – sending the crowd into raptures – Bukayo spent the match dribbling this way and that past Boril, bending in crosses and pressuring the opposition. He was unstoppable!

After a brilliant eighty-five minutes, he was subbed, with Jadon coming on to replace him. The crowd stood as one to applaud Bukayo. The game finished 1-0, but the millions of people watching at home had found a new young star. He was named Player of the Match!

And his Euro 2020 journey was just beginning. Gareth was so pleased with Bukayo's flair and his work rate that he put him in the team for the next game – a Round of 16 knock-out tie against the mighty Germany!

To have this much trust from the England manager was huge. The whole country would be glued to the match, and 40,000 fans were allowed into Wembley to watch. The atmosphere was electric as the game kicked off. Bukayo had a strong first half, causing all sorts of problems for the defenders. But Germany were tough opponents, and midway through the second half he was replaced. Soon afterwards, Raheem steered home a cross from Luke Shaw. 1-0! Just a few minutes later, Harry powered a header into the net. 2-0! Germany were beaten and Wembley was in wonderland!

Bukayo ran back on to the pitch at full-time to celebrate with his teammates, as the song "Sweet Caroline" echoed around the stadium. The fans and players roared together: "Good times never seemed so good! So good! So good! So good!" What a result!

"Amazing game!" said Harry to the TV interviewer afterwards. "To hear Wembley like this is just a moment none of us will ever forget!"

On to the next round – a tricky quarter-final against Ukraine in Rome. A nasty knock in training meant Bukayo wasn't part of the matchday squad, but he was ecstatic as he watched his teammates win 4-0. Harry scored another two, and Harry Maguire and Jordan Henderson both got goals too.

By now, with England through to a semi-final against Denmark, the nation was well and truly behind the team. Gareth's squad had the perfect mix of older players and younger players, like a big gang of brothers. They loved playing football together and they loved spending time together. And when Bukayo and some of the others were pictured playing on inflatable unicorns in the hotel swimming pool, it just made people like them more!

Bukayo was fit again for the semi-final. It was another hard-fought match, this time in front of 65,000 fans at Wembley. The game was exciting but edgy, and as England and Denmark wrestled for control, the match was poised at 1-1 at half-time. Bukayo put in another lion-hearted performance, but when his energy ran out he was replaced again by Jack in the sixty-ninth minute.

As the game ticked into extra-time, and Bukayo watched from the bench, he knew there would only be one winner. He had faith in his friends. Sure enough, Raheem won a penalty in the one hundred and fourth minute. Yes! Harry stepped up, and although his first shot was saved, he made no mistake with the rebound. That made it 2-1 – and soon England were into the final against Italy!

"It's coming home, it's coming home, it's coming!" sang the fans. "Football's coming home!"

This was sensational. The only time England had won a major tournament, or even reached a final, was way back in 1966 – thirty-five years before Bukayo had been born! Expectation was at fever pitch as the big day approached, and when the players stepped out on to the Wembley turf on Sunday 11 July, the stadium was a cauldron of noise. The team knew that almost every TV in the country would be tuned in to the match.

Gareth's tactics meant Bukayo started on the bench this time. He was bitterly disappointed, but he trusted his manager. Maybe I'll have a chance to make an impact later, he thought. And he'd barely had time to take his seat before Luke Shaw smashed in a shot, putting England ahead. 1-0!

Italy, however, were no pushovers. They equalized in the second half, and as things got anxious for England, Gareth brought on his super sub ... Bukayo. He sprinted on to the grass. His speed brought more zip to the game straight away – it wasn't too long before the Italian captain Giorgio Chiellini had to tug him back by his collar to try and stop him! Yellow card!

But neither side could find a goal. After a full ninety minutes, plus half an hour of extra time, the teams were still level. This meant only one thing: a penalty shoot-out for the trophy.

The five players chosen by Gareth to take penalties for England were all brave, and they carried huge responsibility. The pressure was enormous. The crowd could hardly bear to watch. Would the Three Lions finally win their first trophy for more than half a century?

The shoot-out began. Harry Kane stepped up and scored past the Italian goalkeeper Gianluigi Donnarumma. Yes! So did Harry Maguire. Come on! Next up for England was Marcus, who sent Donnarumma the wrong way but hit the post with his shot. Oh no!

But there was still hope. Italy had missed one too. If England could just score their fourth and fifth penalties, their dreams of victory were alive. Next up was Jadon. "Please score, mate, please score," whispered Bukayo to himself, as Jadon adjusted the ball and the stadium held its breath. "You can do this."

But the shot was kept out. The crowd groaned and sank into their seats, fearing it was all over. Poor Jadon. It gave Italy the chance to win it with the next penalty – but incredibly, Jordan Pickford dived to his right and kept it out!

The nerves were now unbelievable. Who would win the trophy? If England scored the next penalty, they were level. If they didn't, they would lose. People up and down the country watched on, their hearts pounding.

And making the long journey from the halfway line was Bukayo.

The walk seemed to take for ever. When he had come on earlier in the game, Bukayo had thought of his family, and the coaches and teachers who had supported him. Now he just thought about scoring his penalty. His stomach was full of butterflies. As the stadium noise grew louder, he placed the ball on the spot and stepped back.

Every pair of eyes in Wembley looked down at the nineteen-year-old.

He breathed deep and began his run-up.

He hit the ball sweetly, but Donnarumma guessed the right way.

Saved.

THE GOOD, THE BAD
AND THE UGLY

It felt as though all the air had been sucked out of the stadium.

Bukayo stood there, heartbroken, as the Italy players wheeled around the pitch in joy.

The first people to reach him were his teammates, comforting him. Kalvin was there, then Harry, Luke and Raheem. Soon he was surrounded by his England friends. Gareth appeared, giving him a hug. "You should be so proud," he told Bukayo. "You've been an inspiration this tournament."

The hours and days that followed were a blur. When he left the squad the next morning to be with his family, he just needed to recover. But a sad situation had become even sadder. The three players who had missed penalties – Marcus, Jadon and Bukayo – had all received racist abuse on social media. This hurt him so much. After giving everything for his country, he was being targeted by idiots. He didn't deserve this. No one did.

More heartwarming were the messages of support that came flooding in, from Edward Betham Primary School, from Mr Harvey at Greenford High, from his Arsenal teammates and his Hale End coaches, from tens of thousands of proper fans. So much mail arrived for him at the Emirates that the club covered a whole wall in thousands of letters to show Bukayo!

A SPECIAL LETTER

Bukayo received thousands of letters of support after missing his penalty at Euro 2020, but one in particular stood out. It came from a seven-year-old boy from the Isle of Wight called Teddy, who sent Bukayo his pocket money to cheer him up. Teddy wrote: "I hope you are not sad any more. If you was here with me, I would buy you an ice cream from the ice-cream van with my pocket money and we would play football in the park, and I would let you win. But really you would beat me because you are so good. Even Father Christmas knows how good you are because he got me the Arsenal kit with your name on it." Bukayo was so moved by the letter that he invited Teddy and his family to visit the Emirates Stadium, then played football with Teddy on the pitch!

It meant everything to him. On social media, he posted a long and emotional message. "I was hurting so much … For those who have sent me heartfelt letters and wished me and my family well, I'm so thankful. This is what football should be about. There is no place for racism or hate of any kind in football or any area of society … Love always wins."

In a pre-season friendly against Tottenham Hotspur

– Arsenal's fiercest rivals – he was stunned when the Spurs fans gave him a big round of applause to show their support. It was clear to Bukayo that he had millions of people on his side, and as the season began again, he turned his attention back to helping Arsenal.

And as always, he did it in style. The goals he scored were superb: a stunner against West Brom, a side-foot strike against Spurs, a close-range blast against Newcastle, two left-footed missiles against Norwich. By Christmas he was flying, and the goals kept coming in the New Year. A neat finish against Manchester City, a piledriver against Watford and – just months after his Wembley miss – confident penalties against Chelsea and Manchester United.

But Bukayo always offered far more than goals. His energy and enthusiasm were infectious, both on the pitch and in the changing room. By the end of the season, he had racked up forty-three appearances, twelve goals and seven assists, which saw him named Arsenal's Player of the Season for the second time in a row. As if that wasn't enough, he was also nominated for both the Premier League Young Player of the Season and the Premier League Player of the Season!

Had Bukayo recovered from his penalty

heartbreak? You bet he had! Little Chilli was back.

But he knew there was more to come – much more. Although Arsenal had only finished fifth, Mikel was starting to get his young team playing with more passion and unity. There was even talk of some exciting new signings coming in over the summer.

"I'm feeling good about our chances next year," said Eddie to Bukayo, as they practised their shooting at the final training session of the season.

They looked across at their teammates. It was nearly the summer break, but Ben White, Martin Ødegaard, Aaron Ramsdale, Gabriel Magalhães, Granit Xhaka and Gabriel Martinelli looked as determined as ever.

"You're right," said Bukayo. He, too, was desperate to bring success to the Emirates Stadium. "Next season could be the one."

Was there something special brewing at London Colney?

A DREAM
START

Bukayo looked at the Premier League table on his phone and gave a broad smile.

Played five, won five.

It was a month into the 2022-23 season and the Gunners were on fire. Mikel and his players had taken the club to the top of the league – for the first time since 2016!

New signings Gabriel Jesus and Oleksandr Zinchenko, both from Manchester City, had brought more experience to the squad. Bukayo, Martin and Gabriel Martinelli were all fizzing with energy, and players like Ben, William Saliba and Thomas Partey were all strong and dependable. The fans were pouring into the matches, excited. "We've got Super Mik Arteta!" they sang.

Bukayo knew Arsenal's history. The last time Arsenal had won the Premier League was way back in the 2003-04 season. Yomi Senior still spoke to him about the players that had taken the Gunners to the top back then. Maybe this would be the year that the club had new legends to talk about.

Their first setback came in September at Old Trafford, with a 3-1 defeat to Manchester United. But if anything, this just made them more resolved to get back to winning ways. They beat Brentford 3-0 away, then smashed Spurs 3-1 at home in a deafening atmosphere.

Their next big game, however, was against Liverpool. Would Mikel's men stumble again, like they had against United?

Things started well. After just a minute, Bukayo and Martin played in Gabriel Martinelli to score. 1-0! "Yes, Gabi!" shouted Bukayo, as his teammate ran around in delight and the Emirates Stadium erupted. But there were twists to come. First, Liverpool equalized on thirty-four minutes through

Darwin Nuñez. Then, as half-time approached, Arsenal broke fast down the left. The ball was played low across the box, Gabriel Jesus dummied it through his legs… and there was Bukayo to poke it home! 2-1!

The second half was full of tension, particularly after Roberto Firmino finished a tidy Liverpool move to make it 2-2. Both sides pushed for a winner, with 60,000 fans yelling encouragement. But the decisive moment came in the seventy-sixth minute, when Gabriel Jesus was clipped as he tried to meet a cross. Penalty to Arsenal! A chance to take all three points.

Bukayo stepped up and placed the ball on the spot. The Liverpool keeper Alisson stood tall between the posts. Bukayo looked calm as he stared at the ball. But would he score, or would he miss? The answer came two seconds later, when his left boot sent the ball whizzing low to Alisson's right. 3-2! His teammates mobbed him as he ran off to celebrate.

This was a huge win. More victories soon followed, including a tight 1-0 battle against London rivals Chelsea. By mid-November, Arsenal had won fourteen of their sixteen matches in the Premier

League, putting them right at the top of the table. It was a glorious start to the season.

For the next month, however, football had other things to focus on. More than 3,000 miles away, in the country of Qatar, the World Cup was about to begin.

MORE ENGLAND DREAMS

It was the forty-third minute of England's opening match against Iran, and the Khalifa International Stadium was about to witness a world-class finish.

From the left, Luke Shaw floated a corner into the box. It was met by Harry Maguire, who headed the ball towards Bukayo. He let it bounce once, opened up his shoulders, then unleashed a brilliant volley into the net.

"And battered in by Saka!" shouted the TV commentator, as Bukayo ran off to celebrate his first World Cup goal.

He was loving being back with his England

teammates. Almost all the players had also been in the Euro 2020 squad, so the team already had an iron-strong bond – and their confidence showed on the pitch. In the first game, Bukayo bagged two against Iran in a 6-2 win, with Marcus, Jack, Raheem and Jude all scoring too.

He started again in the next match, a cagey 0-0 against the USA, but Gareth gave him a well-earned rest for the third group game, a 3-0 win against Wales. Suddenly, England were back in the knock-out stages of a major tournament. The players were feeling good, the goals were flowing, and the fans back home were sensing something big.

Their next match was in the Round of 16 against Senegal, who had won the Africa Cup of Nations just a year earlier. But England were a high-quality team, with the right blend of experience, power and creativity. They swept Senegal aside 3-0, with Bukayo getting the all-important third. The fans in the stadium – and back in England – were delirious with happiness. Gareth Southgate's men were through to the World Cup quarter-final against France, the reigning world champions!

Bukayo was causing a buzz after scoring three

goals in his three games. He was showing football fans all around the world what he could do. Because of this, he was chosen to give a press conference the day after the Senegal match. In a room full of journalists, he was asked if he thought England could win the trophy. Bukayo didn't hesitate. "Of course," he said. "We have to believe we can win it. But right now, our focus is on the next game."

Another journalist spoke about the previous World Cup, which had made a star out of French striker Kylian Mbappé. Did Bukayo see himself as this World Cup's Mbappé? His face broke into a grin. "Thank you for the compliment, but no," he replied politely. "There's only one Kylian Mbappé, and at the same time there's only one me."

Five days later, in front of nearly 70,000 fans, Bukayo's England and Mbappé's France lined up for the national anthems at Qatar's Al Bayt Stadium. This was the big one. A huge banner in the stands had been painted by an England supporter with the words "Football's Coming Home". The television audience numbered hundreds of millions.

France struck first, with young midfielder Aurélien Tchouaméni firing home from the edge of the box. But England stayed calm, and Bukayo looked dangerous whenever he got the ball. On fifty-four minutes, he burst into the box from the right, side-stepped a defender and was brought down. Penalty to England – and captain Harry Kane blasted it into the net! 1-1!

But things were moving fast. Twenty minutes later, Olivier Giroud headed in an Antoine Griezmann cross to put France ahead. Noooo! 2-1 down! Bukayo, who had played his heart out, was substituted soon afterwards. He now had to watch from the sides, exhausted, desperately hoping for an England equalizer.

Their chance came on eighty-two minutes, when Mason Mount ran on to a through-ball. But before he could reach it, he was bundled to the grass in the box. Surely a foul? The referee checked the monitor. Another penalty to England! Gareth punched the air. The fans roared. If this went in, it would be 2-2. Their hopes would be alive!

Harry took the ball. From the substitutes' bench, Bukayo held his breath and looked on. He knew exactly how his captain would be feeling.

Harry paused, ran up and shot. The ball went

speeding over the bar and into the stands. He'd missed. On the pitch, Mbappé and his teammates celebrated the moment as though France had scored a goal.

Just minutes later, the final whistle blew. The England players fell to their knees.

For Bukayo, Harry, Gareth and the rest of the squad, their World Cup journey was over.

CHASING THE
PREMIER LEAGUE

Bukayo was devastated after Qatar, but he knew he had a task to finish at home. Arsenal were soon back into the flow of the Premier League season – and Bukayo was soon back in the action, first helping the team to a 2-0 win at Spurs then firing in a wondergoal as the Gunners beat Manchester United 3-2.

In the changing room after the United game, Bukayo and Eddie – the two former Hale End boys – were overjoyed. "We were right," Bukayo said to his friend, who had scored Arsenal's other goals. "This really could be our season!"

Everything was looking good. Mikel had just been named Manager of the Month in the Premier League and Arsenal were five points clear of Manchester City, their nearest rivals. They'd even been able to strengthen their squad in January, buying Leandro Trossard from Brighton and Jorginho from Chelsea. Come on, you Gunners!

But as the weeks ticked by, the pressure started to show. They were still playing with guts and skill, but their standards were slipping. They lost to Everton, then – oh no! – to City. "Stay focused, boys!" Mikel urged his players. "Stay focused!"

Arsenal had to move up a gear – and they did. They won each of their next seven games, with Bukayo banging in four goals along the way. But City were still hot on their heels. And when April arrived, Arsenal had another hiccup. They drew three matches in a row, dropping valuable points.

Their next game was a must-win against City, but a disastrous day saw them lose 4-1 to their title rivals. Suddenly, the Premier League was slipping away. They battled hard, desperate not to lose out – but City just kept on winning their games.

By mid-May, they couldn't be caught. Arsenal

would be finishing second.

Bukayo and the squad were absolutely gutted. This was supposed to have been their season, the year they brought the title back to the Emirates Stadium. But as City lifted the trophy up in Manchester, among fireworks and confetti, the Arsenal players could only dream of the future.

EPILOGUE

LOOKING AHEAD

On a summer's evening, Old Trafford was packed to the rafters.

It was just a few weeks after the end of the season, and twenty-one-year-old Bukayo was back on the pitch. England were playing North Macedonia in a qualifier for Euro 2024, and he was in the starting line-up.

He tried to forget the Premier League disappointment. Just a few weeks ago, he'd signed a new four-year contract with Arsenal. Nothing could have made him happier.

Tonight, meanwhile, was a chance to play with

freedom and enjoyment in front of 70,000 fans. Lift-off came in the thirty-fourth minute, when Kyle Walker played the ball into his feet. He took two touches then sent a thunderbolt into the roof of the net. Yesssss!

At the start of the second half he went one better, running on to a long ball from Trent Alexander-Arnold before leathering a thirty-yard volley past the keeper. The stadium exploded with noise. WOW!

And was there more to come? Of course there was. Just two minutes later, a brilliant pass from Harry Kane set Bukayo free. He sped into the area and calmly slotted it into the goal. YESSS! A HAT-TRICK FOR ENGLAND!

He slid on his knees towards the corner flag as the fans went wild.

The Three Lions won the match 7-0. And Bukayo? He was just doing what he loved best. Playing football with a smile on his face.

The future was bright indeed.

Saka's Timeline

5 September 2001	Bukayo Ayoyinka Temidayo Saka is born in Ealing, London.
2007/08	He begins playing for local team Greenford Celtic and soon attracts the attention of scouts from professional clubs.
2008	After a brief trial at Watford, he is invited to train at Arsenal's Hale End academy.
5 May 2010	Aged eight, he signs his first official forms with Arsenal.
2012	He helps Edward Betham Primary School to win the Ealing Peal Shield.

2013	He helps Edward Betham Primary School to win the Ealing Peal Shield – again!
February 2016	He makes his debut for England Under-15s. He will later go on to play for the Under-16s, the Under-17s, the Under-18s, the Under-19s, the Under-21s and the full national team.
May 2018	He helps England Under-17s get to the semi-finals of the Under-17 European Championships.
Summer 2018	He leaves Greenford High School with four A*s and three As in his GCSEs.
September 2018	He signs his first full-time contract with Arsenal, days after his 17th birthday.
29 November 2018	He makes his first-team debut for Arsenal, coming on as a substitute in a Europa League match against Vorskla Poltava in Ukraine.

13 December 2018	He makes his full debut for Arsenal, in a Europa League match against Qarabag at the Emirates Stadium.
1 January 2019	He makes his Premier League debut, coming on as a substitute in a match against Fulham.
29 May 2019	He is an unused substitute as Arsenal win the 2019 Europa League Final against Chelsea.
19 September 2019	He scores his first goal for the Arsenal first team, in a 3-0 win over Eintracht Frankfurt. He also gets two assists.
1 July 2020	He signs a contract extension with Arsenal.
1 August 2020	He is an unused substitute as Arsenal win the 2020 FA Cup Final against Chelsea.
29 August 2020	He starts for Arsenal in their FA Community Shield win against Liverpool.

8 October 2020	He makes his debut for the England senior team, starting in a 3-0 win over Wales.
2 June 2021	He scores his first goal for England, in a 1-0 win over Austria in a friendly.
4 June 2021	He is named Arsenal Player of the Season.
June/July 2021	He is part of the England squad for Euro 2020. After performing brilliantly in the tournament, he misses England's fifth penalty in a shoot-out in the final. He is abused online, but receives huge support from proper football fans.
8 June 2022	After a brilliant season, he is named Arsenal Player of the Season for the second time.
23 September 2022	Continuing his strong performances for the Three Lions, he is named England Men's Player of the Year.

November/ December 2022	He is part of the England squad for the 2022 UEFA World Cup in Qatar, scoring three goals as England get to the quarter-finals.
13 March 2023	After another amazing year, he is named Men's Young Player of the Year at the London Football Awards.
23 May 2023	To the delight of Gunners fans, he signs a new long-term contract with Arsenal.
29 May 2023	He is named PFA Young Player of the Year, after helping Arsenal finish in second place in the Premier League.
19 June 2023	He scores his first hat-trick, as England beat North Macedonia in a qualifier for Euro 2024.
5 September 2023	He is named England Men's Player of the Year for the second year running.
20 September 2023	He makes his Champions League debut, scoring in a 4-0 home win over PSV Eindhoven.

Honours for
Club and Country

FA Cup winner:	2020
FA Community Shield winner:	2023, 2020
Europa League runner-up:	2019
European Championship runner-up:	2020

Individual
Honours

England Men's Player of the Year:	2021-22
England Men's Player of the Year:	2022-23
Arsenal Player of the Season:	2021-22, 2020-21
Premier League Player of the Month:	March 2023

Fun Bukayo Facts!

His full name is Bukayo Ayoyinka Temidayo Saka.

He once had a Facetime call from American celebrity Kim Kardashian and her football-loving son!

Because Bukayo's parents had moved to England from Nigeria, he could have played international football for Nigeria. But because he has always lived in England, he chose to represent his home country.

He once said that the toughest opponent he'd ever faced was his England teammate Kyle Walker, who played against Bukayo for Manchester City.

His favourite player of all-time is Arsenal's legendary French striker, Thierry Henry.

Before the 2022 World Cup, Bukayo and the England squad took inspiration from England's Women's Team, the Lionesses, who had won the European Championships a few months earlier. "They made some history, a lot of history," he said. "I feel like there's always fire in the belly, but seeing them do it... We're all so proud. And we want to do it as well."

His nicknames are Little Chilli and Starboy.

When asked what he would be if he wasn't a footballer, Bukayo once said that if he was a little bit taller, he would have been a basketballer!

Another of his heroes is Ian Wright, the Arsenal striker who scored 128 times for the Gunners in 221 appearances – including eleven hat-tricks!

BUKAYO'S FAVOURITE THINGS

Bukayo once gave an interview with the British magazine GQ, where he was asked to name the ten things he couldn't live without. Here's what he chose!

His **tablet**: "I use it to watch things when we're on the road. My essential apps are YouTube, Netflix and Instagram. And I always watch clips of the opposition before a game, to try to understand the way they play."

His **portable speaker**: "I love music so I use it all the time. Most of the songs I listen to are Afrobeat songs. Music makes you feel good – it makes you happy; it makes you want to smile and dance."

Twix bars: "They're my favourite chocolate bar. I just love them."

His **PlayStation controller**: "I play FIFA, Call of Duty, sometimes NBA Basketball too. I played FIFA against my teammate Eddie Nketiah and scored a hat-trick. I think I'm the best gamer in the team."

A football: "Football's my life. It's happiness for me. Every time you get on the pitch, every time I touch a football, I forget about any problems or issues. I've always been in love with football."

A family photo: "Family means everything to me. My family's been a very important influence on my career, always there for me, always encouraging me. But I consider my whole team as a family. This is the best way to feel about each other if you want to achieve."

Cocoa butter: "I use it every day. It's good for my skin. It keeps me moisturized and it smells good."

His bible: "It's really special to me. I try to read it every night before I go to bed. I've learnt a lot from it. Religion's a big part of my life – I'm a strong believer in God."

His comb: "It's always with me. It keeps my hair fresh, especially when I haven't had a haircut in a while. It's always in my pocket or washbag."

White trainers: "I'll wear white trainers with anything, even a suit. Whatever I'm wearing that day, I can put them on and I'll feel confident."

LEGENDARY ARSENAL
NUMBER SEVENS

Wearing the Arsenal number seven shirt has been one of the biggest privileges of Bukayo's career. Here are four other superstars who came before him.

Liam Brady (1973-1980)
235 games for Arsenal, forty-three goals
This left-footed Irish midfielder was famed for his passing and tackling. When he retired as a footballer, he spent almost twenty years as head of Arsenal's youth development.

David Rocastle (1985-1992)
218 games for Arsenal, twenty-four goals
London-born midfielder and winger David "Rocky"

Rocastle was adored by the Arsenal fans. He died tragically young, at just thirty-three, and his name is still displayed at the Emirates Stadium.

Robert Pires (2000-2006)
189 games for Arsenal, sixty-two goals
This flying Frenchman was one of Arsenal's key players in their glory years under manager Arsène Wenger. He also won the 1998 World Cup and Euro 2000 with France.

Alexis Sánchez (2014-2018)
122 games for Arsenal, sixty goals
This strong Chilean forward helped Arsenal to win two FA Cups, and his skill made him one of Bukayo's favourite players. At Hale End, Bukayo even tried to wear the same boots as him!

UNICORN FUN

When Bukayo was pictured jumping into a swimming pool on top of an inflatable unicorn at Euro 2020, people on the internet turned it into a fun meme.

They took the photo of Bukayo and his unicorn and put them in other funny situations, like flying across the moon with ET, jumping over a fence in a horse race, and even soaring through the air with the Avengers!

Bukayo's Clubs

ARSENAL FOOTBALL CLUB

Founded: 1886

Previous Names: Dial Square, Royal Arsenal, Woolwich Arsenal

Nickname: The Gunners

Most appearances: David O'Leary (722 appearances)

All-time Top Scorer: Thierry Henry (228 goals)

Ground: Emirates Stadium (capacity 60,704)

Previous ground: Highbury (from 1913 to 2006)

ARSENAL'S RECORDS AND HONOURS:

League champions: thirteen times (2003/04, 2001/02, 1997/98, 1990/91, 1988/89, 1970/71, 1952/53, 1947/48, 1937/38, 1934/35, 1933/34, 1932/33, 1930/31)

FA Cup winners: fourteen times (2020 v Chelsea; 2017 v Chelsea; 2015 v Aston Villa; 2014 v Hull City; 2005 v Manchester United; 2003 v Southampton; 2002 v Chelsea; 1998 v Newcastle United; 1993 v Sheffield Wednesday; 1979 v Manchester United; 1971 v Liverpool; 1950 v Liverpool; 1936 v Sheffield United; 1930 v Huddersfield Town)

League Cup winners: twice (1993 v Sheffield Wednesday; 1987 v Liverpool)

European Fairs Cup winners: once (1970 v Anderlecht)

UEFA Cup Winners' Cup: once (1994 v Parma)

Charity Shield/ Community Shield winners: fourteen times, plus one shared (2023 v Manchester City; 2020 v Liverpool; 2017 v Chelsea; 2015 v Chelsea; 2014 v Manchester City; 2004 v Manchester United; 2002 v Liverpool; 1999 v Manchester United; 1998 v Manchester United; 1991 v Tottenham Hotspur (shared); 1953 v Blackpool; 1948 v Manchester United; 1938 v Preston North End; 1934 v Manchester City; 1933 v Everton; 1931 v West Bromwich Albion; 1930 v Sheffield Wednesday)

ARSENAL'S INVINCIBLES

Bukayo was just a toddler when the 2003-04 season kicked off – but it was the greatest in Arsenal's history.

Over a thirty-eight-game Premier League season, they won twenty-six games and drew twelve, finishing top of the table without a single defeat, eleven points clear of second-placed Chelsea. To be champions of England is always special – but to be champions without losing a game was even more exceptional.

The team are now known as "The Invincibles". They scored more goals than any of their rivals (seventy-three), conceded fewer (twenty-six), and were given a specially made golden trophy to mark their amazing achievement.

The mastermind behind the team was manager

Arsène Wenger, but he was blessed with an incredible squad of players. These included goalkeeper Jens Lehmann, defenders Ashley Cole, Sol Campbell, Lauren and Kolo Touré, midfielders Robert Pires, Patrick Vieira, Gilberto Silva, Freddie Ljungberg and Ray Parlour, and forwards Dennis Bergkamp and Thierry Henry.

Thierry scored thirty goals, making him the top scorer in the league.

When the team won the trophy, they paraded it through the streets of North London to Islington Town Hall. Around a quarter of a million fans came out to cheer them on!

APPEARANCES
FOR ENGLAND

Bukayo has played for England Under-15s (four games, one goal), England Under-16s (six games, one goal), Under-17s (nine games, one goal), Under-18s (five games, one goal), Under-19s (ten games, four goals) and Under-21s (one game, no goals).

But his proudest moments have come while playing for the senior team. At the start of the 2023/24 season, he had played twenty-eight times, scoring eleven goals and appearing in two major tournaments.

When he scored his first hat-trick for the Three Lions against North Macedonia in 2023, he summed up how much it meant to him. "There's nothing I can say to really describe how I'm feeling right now," he said. "I can't really put it into words. I'm just so happy."

Also available in the Football Legends series:

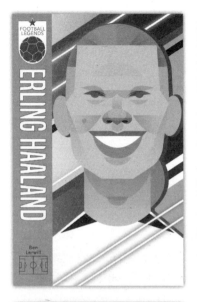

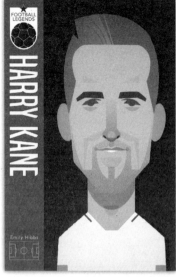

FOOTBALL LEGENDS

TAMMY ABRAHAM

Matt Whyman

KYLIAN MBAPPÉ

Ed Hawkins

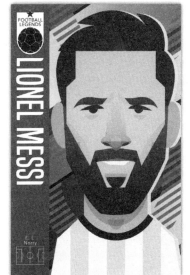

FOOTBALL LEGENDS

LIONEL MESSI

E. L. Norry

FOOTBALL LEGENDS

GARETH SOUTHGATE

E. L. Norry